PICK A PEPPER

A Photographic Guide to Chile Peppers, Their History, and Uses

By Jason Logsdon
Edited By Gary Logsdon
Presented By ChilePeppersRecipes.com

Copyright © 2011 by Primolicious LLC

All rights reserved. Printed in the United States of America. No part of this book may be used or reproduced in any manner whatsoever without written permission except in the case of brief quotations embodied in critical articles and reviews.

For more information please contact Primolicious LLC at 12 Pimlico Road, Wolcott CT 06716.

Cover Photo Credits: www.flickr.com/photos/johnwinkelman

Back Cover Photo Credits:
    http://www.flickr.com/photos/notahipster
    http://www.flickr.com/photos/jkohen
    http://www.flickr.com/photos/azadam
    http://commons.wikimedia.org

ISBN-13: 978-1460995747
ISBN-10: 1460995740

To Jodi and Barb,
Thanks for spicing up our lives

TABLE OF CONTENTS

Introduction 1	Malagueta 42
Aji 2	Manzano 44
Anaheim 4	Mirasol 46
Ancho 6	Mulato 48
Arbol (de Arbols)............8	Naga Jolokia 50
Bird's Eye 10	Naga Viper....................52
Cascabel 12	New Mexico 54
Cayenne 14	Pasilla 56
Cherry 16	Pequin 58
Chiltepin........................18	Poblano 60
Chipotle 20	Red Savina Habanero .62
Dundicut 22	Rocotillo 64
Fatalii.............................24	Santaka 66
Fresno 26	Scotch Bonnet.............68
Guajillo 28	Serrano 70
Guntur Sannam 30	Tabasco 72
Habanero 32	Thai................................74
Hungarian Yellow Wax.34	Tien Tsin 76
Jalapeno 36	Yatsufusa 78
Kashmiri........................38	Scoville Scale 80
Korean 40	Photo Credits 81

Introduction

Chile peppers have long fascinated people and are thought to have been consumed by humans as far back as 7500BC. They originated in the Americas and once discovered by explorers quickly spread throughout the world. Chiles spread by many means ranging from European explorers and merchants to the Africans ensnared in the slave trade.

As the chile peppers changed and evolved they became very important in local cuisines and assumed lofty places in the culture of many countries. Some cuisines are known for their use of peppers like Jamaican jerk seasonings, Mexican Chiles en Nogada, early American Creole, and the ever present Indian curries.

Here is a look at 39 different chile peppers. Some, like the jalapeno, are well known and common while others are obscure and specific to their region. Some are mild like the Anaheim and some are so hot they are literally being used as weapons. Regardless of the properties, each one of these peppers plays an important part in at least one culture around the world.

We hope you enjoy learning about all of these exciting peppers!

**For more information, recipes, and pepper forums please visit our companion website:
www.chilepeppersrecipes.com**

AJI

Pronunciation: ah-hee
Length: 4 - 6"
Width: ½ - 1 ½"
Scientific Name: Capsicum baccatum
Other Names: peruvian puff pepper, pimiento chile
Scoville Range: 30,000+

Origin and History

The aji pepper dates back thousands of years to the Moche culture in Peru. In the wild the plant is most common in the mountains of South America, especially Bolivia. Aji is a mainstay of Peruvian cooking. Although it can grow in the southern United States, it is uncommon in super markets in this country, but is increasingly available at specialty markets.

Description

Aji fruits are typically orange or red and sometimes yellow or purple, and average 40 pods per plant. Shapes vary, but they are typically elongated or tapered. They have white or green flowers with green or gold corollas. Aji plants are more tolerant of cool weather than many other pepper plants.

The subtle bouquet of this hot spicy pepper varies among the many cultivars. Aji limo, for example, has a clear citrus flavor with the aroma of lemons and limes and a strong hint of citron. Aji amarillo is a yellow chile with a distinguished fruity taste sometimes described as grassy. Aji mirasol is the dried form of Aji amerillo. Aji panca has a berry-like fruity flavor and an aromatic, smoky taste.

"Aji" is also used as a general term for peppers in South America.

How to Serve or Use

Aji pepper infuses food with a unique fruity taste. Papas a la Huancaina, tamales, ceviche, arroz con pollo, and many other South American dishes use aji chiles. Aji de gallino is a traditional Argentinean dish of chicken in a spicy yellow chile pepper sauce. Peruvian causa combines aji amarillo sauce and potatoes with tuna, crab, or chicken in a layered dish.

Aji is a major ingredient in chimichurri, a condiment widely used in dishes in Argentina and Uruguay. Argentinean cuisine uses chimichurri as a sauce or marinade with grilled steak, fish, or chicken. The basic ingredients are fresh parsley, oregano, garlic, oil, vinegar, and chile pepper flakes, but there are many regional variations.

Aji peppers are also dried and ground into colorful powders, used fresh in salsa and salads, made into paste, or pickled. Often times cooks reconstitute dried aji chiles when they cannot find fresh ones.

ANAHEIM

Pronunciation: an-uh-hahym
Length: 3 - 8"
Width: ~1"
Scientific Name: Capsicum annuum
Other Names: california pepper, magdelena,
New Mexico peppers
Scoville Range: 500 - 2,500

ORIGIN AND HISTORY

During the early part of the twentieth century, Emilio Ortega brought the seeds that would become known as the Anaheim pepper to the region of Anaheim, California. The original variety of this pepper was actually from New Mexico and are occasionally referred to as New Mexico peppers. It is important to note, however, that the New Mexico variety is actually quite a bit hotter and rates significantly higher on the Scoville scale.

Anaheim peppers are sometimes referred to as chile peppers, though they are not nearly as hot as most chile peppers. The Anaheim pepper is often dried as chile seco del norte.

DESCRIPTION

The Anaheim pepper has many similar traits and characteristics of the traditional chile pepper. As it matures to full ripeness, the Anaheim pepper will turn from green to a bright red. It also reaches its peak rating on the Scoville scale when it is fully ripe.

The pepper is generally between 3 and 8 inches long and less than 1 inch in width. They grow on productive plants about 2 feet tall and take almost 80 days to reach full maturity.

HOW TO SERVE OR USE

Many subtle dishes call for using the Anaheim pepper because its mild flavor won't overwhelm the other spices and flavoring used to make up the dish. It is ideal for salads and adds a nice, light spice to them.

They are also commonly stuffed for a mild version of chile rellenos or dipped in an egg and flour mixture then fried.

Because of thier subtle flavor they are a very versitle pepper that can be used around people who aren't very fond of heat.

ANCHO

Pronunciation: AHN-choh
Length: 4"
Width: 3"
Scientific Name: Capsicum annuum
Other Names: mulato chile, black chile
Scoville Range: 1,000 - 1,500

ORIGIN AND HISTORY

The ancho is a popular chile grown in Mexico made from dried poblano chiles. The pepper is harvested from a bush with multiple stems that can grow up to 25 inches tall. The word Ancho means wide, which refers to the flat heart shape that tapers to a point at the bottom of the poblano chile. Varieties of ancho include light brown and black mulato chiles.

The ancho chile is used in the symbolic Mexican dish known as Chiles en Nogada. This dish is served during Mexican independence holidays as part of a meal that incorporates the Mexican flag colors green, white and red.

DESCRIPTION

The pod of the ancho begins as a dark purple and then ripens to a bright red color. When it is dried the color turns to blackish brown. The skin of the ancho has a smooth waxy texture but it is actually quite tough. The pepper has to be soaked longer than other chiles in order to soften the skin.

The ancho chile is sweet and slightly fruity like raisins. It smells a bit like prunes and has a mild to medium heat. Ancho chiles contain more pulp than other chiles. Anchos are commonly used to make Mexican style sauces.

HOW TO SERVE OR USE

Ancho is sold as a chile powder, a puree, and packaged as dried pods. It is a staple ingredient in red chile and tamales. They are often stuffed and fried with an egg coating. Ancho can also be used to make a paste for use as a marinade for meat or vegetables. The mellow flavor also makes it a favorite ingredient in salsa. Anchos can be made into a relish and used as a condiment for Mexican dishes. Dried anchos are also served crumbled over soup as a spicy and fruity garnish.

Anchos should be roasted and peeled before canning or preserving. Removing the skin improves the texture of the chile. They can be frozen in airtight containers for several months for up to one year. Most recipes call for soaking frozen or preserved anchos in hot water for half an hour before using.

ARBOL (DE ARBOLS)

Pronunciation: day-ar-boll
Length: 2 - 3"
Width: ½ - 3/8"
Scientific Name: Capsicum annuum
Other Names: bird's beak chile, rat's tail chile
Scoville Range: 15,000 - 60,000

Origin and History

Chile de arbol has its origin in the Mexican states of Oaxaca and Jalisco. The name means "tree like" in Spanish and was obtained from the tall plants from which it grows. These plants can grow to over 5 feet in height. Arbol chile is a member of the nightshade family and related to cayenne pepper.

Arbol chile is grown around the world. In the northern hemisphere it is planted in March and harvested in August and September. Southern hemisphere gardeners plant the pepper in July through October and harvest in February. The arbol chile is hardy and easy to grow.

Description

The chiles start out green and then turn bright red when they are mature. They have a narrow curved shape, tapered to a point at the bottom with a woody stem.

Arbol have a strong heat and smoky, acidic flavor. They add extra heat, more than flavor, to sauces and dishes.

The bright red color of the arbol chile does not fade even after it is dried. The pods are used in holiday wreaths. After harvesting, chiles are strung to dry in decorative arrangements called ristras. The ristra is hung in the front of the home as a welcome and to bring good fortune.

How to Serve or Use

The peppers are commonly available fresh, dried, or in powdered form. In addition to Mexican cuisine, arbol chile is an important ingredient in Thai curry.

The ground powder of the chile is used to season salsas, hot sauces, and soups. It is also sprinkled on raw vegetables. The dried pods of the arbols chile are also used to flavor oil and vinegar.

The arbol chile is not appropriate for pickling because it has very little flesh. However, it is very good for adding extra heat to other pickled vegetables. In Mexico, arbol chiles are fried whole or roasted until crisp and served with black beans. One popular table salsa calls for tomatillos, garlic, onion and toasted arbol chile.

Bird's Eye

Pronunciation: burdz-ahy
Length: 1"
Width: Less than 1"
Scientific Name: Capsicum frutescens
Other Names: birdseye, piri piri, kochchi, cili padi, cabe rawit
Scoville Range: 50,000 - 100,000

ORIGIN AND HISTORY

There are actually several varieties of peppers throughout the world commonly referred to as bird's eye peppers, such as the chiltepin pepper from the southern regions of the United States, Mexico, and Central America.

The true bird's eye pepper hails from regions of Southeast Asia, namely Cambodia, Laos, Vietnam, Thailand, Malaysia, Singapore, and the Philippines. This species can also be found in regions of India, especially Kerala.

DESCRIPTION

The bird's eye chili plant produces small fruits that taper from the stem to their end and often grow 2 to 3 peppers per node. The colors of the bird's eye peppers tend to be mostly red, though they are also commonly seen as yellow, black, and even purple. While the bird's eye pepper is relatively small its heat is quite intense.

In fact, at one time the bird's eye pepper was listed in the Guinness Book of World Records as the world's hottest pepper.

The plant height can reach about 6 feet tall, though some varieties are smaller, especially the more ornamental varieties.

HOW TO SERVE OR USE

The bird's eye pepper is commonly used as a spice in a variety of dishes in Filipino, Indonesian, Laotian, Thai, Malaysian, and Vietnamese cuisines. It is what gives these dishes their signature fiery zest. The bird's eye pepper can also be added to vinegar to give it extra flavor. The leaves of the plant are also used in salads and other garnishments.

The bird's eye is often found in Kerala cuisine, even in Sambharam, a buttermilk-type drink flavored with chiles and ginger. It is also a main ingredient in kochchi sambal which is a salad made from fresh coconut ground with Thai chillies and lime juice. It is often used in the Filipino dishes of bicol express, a stew, and tinola, a chicken soup which uses the leaves.

The pepper also has medicinal uses and has been used traditionally to ease arthritis and rheumatism, and as a cure for upset stomachs, flatulence, and toothache. When mixed with water is also acts as a natural insect repellent and pesticide.

CASCABEL

Pronunciation: kas-kah-BELL
Length: 1 - 2"
Width: 1 - 2"
Scientific Name: Capsicum annuum
Other Names: chile bola, rattle chile
Scoville Range: 1,000 - 5,000

Origin and History

The cascabel chile grows in several states on the Pacific coast of Mexico; which include Jalisco, Durango and Coahuila. The chile's name, which means "rattle," refers to the sound that the loose seeds in the dried pepper make when it is shaken.

The cascabel chile is a cultivar of capsicum annuum species. A cultivar is a plant that has been specifically cultivated and selected for certain characteristic such as color, yield and resistance to disease.

Description

Cascabel chiles are smooth round peppers that are similar in size to a hot cherry pepper. When dried, the thick flesh is a deep red to brown in color.

The shell has a medium to low heat and is slightly acidic. The seeds range from moderately hot to hot with a slightly smoky flavor. Cascabel chiles develop a rich nutty taste when they are toasted. They are often preferred to flavor Mexican dishes without adding a lot of heat.

How to Serve or Use

Cascabel chiles can be purchased whole, dried, or pureed. Powdered cascabel is not readily available since the small size of the chile compared to its waste, including seeds and stems, makes it expensive to produce. Dried, whole cascabel chiles are easy to find. The chile is usually toasted and then ground to use for flavor or as a garnish for stews, sauces and soups.

Cascabel chiles can also be hydrated and used as an ingredient of mole sauce. The sauce is used to add flavor to beans, meat and chicken. It is also a spicy addition to enchiladas or tacos. Cascabel chile is also commonly combined with garlic, cumin and other spices to make marinades for shrimp, chicken or beef. For glazes, the flavor of the chile works well to balance the flavor of honey.

Dried chiles placed in airtight containers can last up to six months if stored in a dry, cool, and dark area.

Cayenne

Pronunciation: kahy-en
Length: 2 - 5"
Width: ½"
Scientific Name: Capsicum annuum
Other Names: guinea spice, cow horn pepper, aleva, bird pepper, red pepper
Scoville Range: 30,000 - 50,000

Origin and History

The word "cayenne" comes from the city and river of that name in the country of French Guiana. Cayenne is native to Central and South America and East Africa; it was a major food of the Aztec and Mayan people thousands of years ago. Cayenne peppers now grow in many tropical and sub-tropical areas of the world, including Zanzibar, India, Mexico, and in the warm regions of the United States.

Description

Cayenne plants are 2 to 4 feet tall and bear slender, aromatic, wrinkled pods that are hot, pungent, and biting. The flowers are yellow or white, and are often drooping. The long hollow pods turn bright red, green, orange, or yellow when ripe.

Most cayenne chiles go into making ground cayenne. The commercially available cayenne pepper spice may actually consist of peppers from a variety of plants. In some uses "cayenne" refers to hot peppers in general.

How to Serve or Use

Cayenne has both culinary and medicinal uses. Dried flakes or powder are popular components of hot sauces and are made from the fruit and sometimes the seeds. They are sometimes also sprinkled over sauces to add a little heat like with a hollandaise sauce.

Cayenne has the same heat intensity as Tabasco sauce. Cooks may substitute cayenne for Tabasco to get the pure heat without the extra vinegar. The powder and flakes provide heat in a wide range of dishes from a variety of cuisines. Cayenne spices go well with cheese, eggs, corn, shellfish, onions, peppers, potatoes, rice, tomatoes?and many other foods. Because of its heat, cayenne should be used sparingly, and not confused with paprika or chili powder.

Cayenne is a popular herbal remedy for improving blood circulation, lowering cholesterol, and helping heal ulcers, and has many other healing properties. The capsicum in cayenne is also an effective painkiller. Cayenne powder is high in vitamin A, contains vitamins C, B1, and B2, is low in cholesterol and sodium, and is a very good source of dietary fiber. As an herbal remedy, cayenne comes in the form of extracts, tinctures, powder, capsules, and creams. The lemonade diet, a dietary cleanse, is a mix of cayenne powder, lemon juice, and maple syrup.

Cherry

Pronunciation: CHAIR-ree
Length: 1 - 2"
Width: 1 - 2"
Scientific Name: Capsicum annuum
Other Names: Hungarian cherry pepper, cherry bomb pepper
Scoville Range: 100 - 3,500

ORIGIN AND HISTORY

The cherry pepper traces its origins back thousands of years to Mexico, Central America, and South America. It reached England from the West Indies in the mid 1700s.

DESCRIPTION

The small, round fruits are the size of cherry tomatoes, hence the name. The bright red fruit has sweetness and a moderately mild to medium heat. Each pod is full of many seeds, which are hotter than the flesh. The compact, bushy plants reach about 3 feet high, and have thin, oval dark green leaves on stiff stems. Cherry peppers have thick flesh, making them unsuitable for drying.

HOW TO SERVE OR USE

Cherry peppers are the perfect size for pickling and brining which are very popular uses in Hungarian cuisine. The thick walls of the cherry chile absorb the pickling juice and enrich the flavor. In fact, the most common commercial use of this chile is pickled in brine.

Hungarian cooks also smoke whole peppers, giving them a rich, smoky flavor and meaty character. Smoked cherry peppers are only recently available in the U.S.

The round chiles can be sliced for fresh salsa or combined with tomatillos in salsa verde. Cherry peppers perform well in three-bean salad, on pizza, and in sweet and sour dishes. They make colorful accompaniments to sandwiches and salads.

Cherry pepper jelly goes well with cream cheese and crackers as an appetizer. It also provides a pleasant kick as a glaze on pork.

Cherry peppers lend themselves to being stuffed. Filled with cheese and sometimes sausage, battered, and fried in oil, they are called cherry poppers. Cherry pepper shooters are an Italian-American antipasto dish that involves wrapping aged provolone cheese in a slice of prosciutto and stuffing it into a pickled cherry pepper.

While most recipes use red cherry peppers, people do eat fresh peppers while they are still green, and less hot.

Because they are compact, cheerful, and colorful, cherry pepper plants are also used in ornamental plantings, often in decorative containers on patios and in small gardens. Pepper plants that are sold for ornamental use may have been treated with chemicals that make the fruits unsafe to eat.

Chiltepin

Pronunciation: Ch-ill-teh-pin
Length: less than ½" diameter
Width: less than ½" diameter
Scientific Name: Capsicum annuum
Other Names: chilitepe or chili tepin
Scoville Range: 50,000 - 100,000

Origin and History

The chiltepin pepper, which is also commonly spelled chili tepin pepper, originated in the southern portion of the United States, mainly in Texas, Arizona, and Florida. It grows wild throughout the south and also is common to the Bahamas, Mexico, Central America, and Columbia.

Chiltepin is considered the only wild chile plant in the United States and has a long history here. The peppers are even protected in Coronado National Forest, Big Bend National Park and Organpipe Cactus National Monument. It's sometimes known as the "Mother of All Peppers" and the name "Tepin" comes from a Nahuatl word that means "flea," because of its diminutive size.

The chiltepin pepper was the official pepper of the state of Texas and is now called "the official native pepper" since the jalapeno took its spot. These pepper plants are quite rugged and generally grow on hard rocky surfaces or steep slopes. This makes finding them and having access to them treacherous.

Description

The chiltepin pepper is quite small, less than ½ inch in diameter. It is a round pepper with a slightly oval shape and is sometimes known by its informal name, the bird's eye pepper. This pepper is extremely hot and in Mexico it is often referred to as arrebatado, which alludes to the rapid and violent heat of the pepper which is intense but also short-lived.

Chiltepin peppers are very pungent but have a smoky flavor.

How to Serve or Use

To achieve the greatest potential of this pepper, it should be served whole, as the nature of its short-lived intensity would be diminished by cutting it open or cooking it. They are often pickled, added to cheeses, or fermented into sauces.

Chiltepin peppers can be dried and used whole as condiments, which is a common practice in Opatas, Sonorans, or Yaqui homes.

CHIPOTLE

Pronunciation: chi-POHT-lay
Length: 1 ½ - 3"
Width: ½ - 1"
Scientific Name: Capsicum annuum
Other Names: chilpotle, chile meco, chile ahumado, tipico, chipotle moritas, chipotle meco
Scoville Range: 5,000 - 10,000

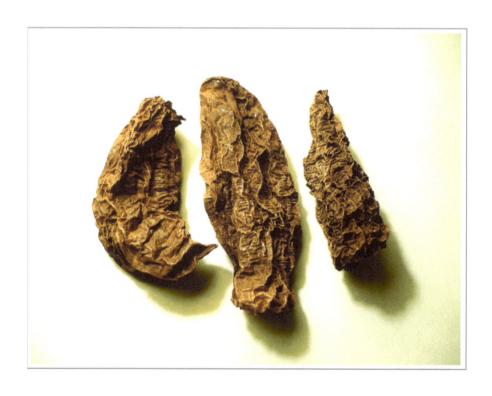

Origin and History

Chipotle peppers originated in central and southern Mexico and spread to North and South America as Mexican food became more popular in the late 20th century. Chipotles are now also grown and processed in Northern Mexico and even into the southern United States to more easily transport to the whole of America.

Chipotles were traditionally made by picking over-ripe and partially dried jalapenos off the plant and then smoking them in a closed smoking chamber on metal grills. They would be smoked for several days and were stirred every few hours.

To speed up production in recent years some growers have begun using large gas dryers or even just adding liquid smoke. Ten pounds of jalapenos will result in about 1 pound of chipotles.

Description

Chipotle peppers are a fiery and smokey chile pepper that imparts an earthy spiciness to any dish they are in. The heat is relatively mild compared to other peppers but is considered hot to the general American public.

The smoking process turns the peppers brown and shrivels them up. There are many varieties of jalapenos that vary in size and heat but most chipotle chiles are produced in the northern Mexican state of Chihuahua. These chiles are known as "morita" which is Spanish for black raspberry or "little purple one" an accurate description of these small, purple peppers.

Another variety of chipotles is chile meco from central and southern Mexico. These peppers are tan and gray in color and resemble a cigar butt. The morita variety is most common in the US as most of the meco are used in Mexico.

How to Serve or Use

Chipotle peppers are used in many different forms including dried chipotle powder, whole chipotle pods, and as cans of chipotle in adobo. Storing chipotles in adobo is a preservation method where whole chipotles are stored in a vinegar based marinade.

Chipotle powder can be used in spice rubs for meats, sprinkled over vegetables, or added to soups or stews. Whole chipotle pods are best used in slow cooked dishes to give the thick flesh time to soften and break down. Chipotles in adobo sauce can be added to just about any dish and any extra can be stored in a ziplock bag in the freezer for later use.

DUNDICUT

Length: ½ - 1"
Width: ½ - 1"
Scientific Name: Capsicum annuum
Other Names: dandicut, lar mirch, dundi cut
Scoville Range: 55,000 - 65,000

Origin and History

The dundicut (or dandicut) pepper is the traditional hot pepper of Pakistan, where it is native. It has been commercially grown in the Tharparkar region of Sindh, Pakistan, and is now widely cultivated.

Dundicut is the red hot pepper used most in Asian cooking.

Description

The heat of the dundicut chile is variable, ranging from medium to hot. Removing the seeds reduces the heat.

The pepper is similar in flavor and appearance to scotch bonnet, but generally not as hot. The flavor is full bodied, fruity, and complex; the fiery flavor is concentrated at the top of the pod. Some chile aficionados describe the aftertaste as being like honeydew melon. Ripe peppers give off a fine aroma, not unlike a good habanero.

The shape of the small pepper ranges from round to teardrop. Ripe peppers are a rich ruby red color.

Some references equate dundicut peppers with dried red chile peppers. They are commercially available whole, crushed, in flakes, and as powder. Dundicut is the major chile commercially grown for powder in Pakistan.

How to Serve or Use

Dundicut peppers are widely used in spicy Thai, Pakistani, and Indian cooking. Cooks use dried dundicut chiles to flavor foods and to marinate meat and shellfish before grilling. When using whole peppers, cooks typically soften the dried peppers before using. One pepper is said to add enough heat and flavor for two servings.

Dundicut peppers are ingredients in pumpkin soup, red chicken curry, and other native dishes of South Asia. These peppers are prime ingredients in certain Southeast Asian curries. Examples include buttermilk curry with dumplings and red chili powder in curry. These chiles are also ingredients in spicy chutney, mustard sauces, and pickled sausage. An unusual recipe uses dundicut peppers to make gefilte fish, a traditional food for the Jewish Passover holiday.

Dundicut chiles are also combined with seeds and fruit to make food for parrots and other birds.

Fatalii

Pronunciation: Fa-TAL-e
Length: 3"
Width: 1 ¼"
Scientific Name: Capsicum chinense
Other Names: fatili
Scoville Range: 125,000 - 325,000

Origin and History

The fatalii chile originates in Central and Southern Africa. It is listed as one of the deadliest hot peppers by the Scoville Food Institute.

Description

Fatalii chile pepper plants can grow up to 4 feet tall. The pod is wide at the top and tapers to a point at the bottom. The peppers start off as a pale green color then mature at around 100 days and turn bright yellow. The skin is wrinkled with a slight sheen.

The extremely hot fatalii has a citrus like flavor in addition to the heat. The fatalii red is another version of this chile and is one of the hottest peppers in the world.

The heat of fatalii is often compared to habanero peppers. Even before they are harvested the heat that the peppers contain is evident from their aroma. Home and commercial gardeners report that the heat from the chile is a deterrent to deer.

How to Serve or Use

Fatalii chiles are combined with fruit to make jellies and jams and combine especially well with peaches. In addition to traditional African dishes, fatalii peppers are used to spice up Mexican dishes like quesadillas. The searing hot pepper has also been added to beer to add a fruity flavor along with heat to the brew. Fatalii chiles are also used to make barbeque sauces, marinades and hot sauce.

As with most peppers, removing the seeds and membranes reduces the heat. It is also advised that contact lenses should be removed and gloves should be worn when handling Fatalii chile peppers.

Fresno

Pronunciation: Frez-noh
Length: 2 - 3"
Width: ~1"
Scientific Name: Capsicum annuum
Other Names: none
Scoville Range: 2,500 - 8,000

Origin and History

The Fresno pepper gets its name from the Fresno region of California where it was first cultivated. It closely resembles the jalapeno pepper but is usually hotter.

The Fresno pepper is most commonly grown in the Southwest region of the United States and many places in Mexico.

Description

The Fresno pepper can be used when green, but is at its ripest peak when it is red. The green peppers are often used to add a mild heat to dishes. Once it turns red the pepper becomes much hotter.

The Fresno pepper has a waxy skin and thick flesh. The pepper itself is generally about 2 to 3 inches long and usually about an inch thick. It has a similar appearance to the jalapeno and serrano peppers.

The Fresno pepper contains more vitamins than the jalapeno, especially Vitamin C. This pepper is also an excellent source of Vitamin B as well as iron, niacin, magnesium, thiamin, and riboflavin. The main drawback of this pepper is that it doesn't dry well and therefore is not ideal for chili powder.

How to Serve or Use

The Fresno pepper is often used in ceviche's or salsas, or in dishes that a jalapeno would be used. Since they do not dry well they are almost always used fresh. They are often used as a garnish in many Tex-Mex dishes.

GUAJILLO

Pronunciation: gwah-HEE-yoh
Length: 3 - 5"
Width: 3"
Scientific Name: Capsicum annuum
Other Names: pulla pepper
Scoville Range: 1,500 - 5,000

Origin and History

The guajillo is among the more common chiles gown in Mexico. Mexican chiles are named according to their shape or taste. The name guajillo means "little gourd." It is an ingredient in Mexican dishes and also in Harissa, a chile paste used in Tunisian cooking.

Description

Guajillo chiles vary in size, which can make them hard to recognize. It is a long pod shaped chile that is able to grow downward (pendant) or upward (erect). The guajillo chile has a thick, smooth leathery skin. It starts out green and then turns reddish brown in color when it matures.

Guajillo chiles have a flavor like green tea with a hint of berry. Their heat is close to jalapenos but with a fruiter and sweeter taste. The chile tends to give a cooked dish a yellowish color. A half ounce serving of guajillo chiles has 50 calories. Based on a 2000 calorie diet each serving provides 190 percent of Vitamin A needed daily.

How to Serve or Use

Guajillo chiles are used in salsas, tamales, soups and sauces. The chile works well with beef and pork. Mint and other herbs are sometimes used to balance the flavor and heat of guajillo chile.

The chile can be purchased dried whole or powdered. Although guajillo chiles are available as a paste, it is best to check the labels carefully as this product may contain unwanted chemicals. Dried chiles should be wiped with a moist towel before cooking to remove soil. They should also be checked for light colored patches that indicate they have been eaten by moth larvae.

To prepare for cooking, tear open the chile to remove the stem, veins and seeds. The chiles can then be soaked and chopped or blended as needed. Some cooks toast the chile in a hot pan before using for extra flavor. Dried guajillo chiles have a shelf life of 3 months.

GUNTUR SANNAM

Pronunciation: Guh-n-ter Say-nah-m
Length: 2 - 6"
Width: Less than 1"
Scientific Name: Capsicum annuum
Other Names: none
Scoville Range: 35,000 - 40,000

ORIGIN AND HISTORY

The Guntur Sannam chili pepper hails from the province of Andhra Pradesh in India. The name is derived from the precise region in which it originated, the Guntur district of Andhra Pradesh, and Sannam means "thin" or "long."

The Guntur Sannam is one of the most popular types of chiles in the world and almost 50% of it is grown in the area. The pepper crops are a vital element of the economic region as it brings in a great deal of money.

Thousands of locals work tirelessly during harvest season to tend the crops and keep up with the ever-growing global demand for these peppers. There was even a pepper research station created near Guntur over 30 years ago to help research cultivation of peppers. There are about 280,000 tonnes of Guntur Sannam peppers harvested each year.

DESCRIPTION

The Guntur Sannam peppers are usually harvested once they have ripened and turned red. They have the appearance of a sweet pea pod, but with a wrinkled and shiny skin that appears as though it has been dried out. They have a deep red color and as they dry they turn even more crimson.

HOW TO SERVE OR USE

One of the biggest uses of Guntur Sannam is to extract the capsaicin from it for use in other products. They are also dried and used in chile powders and spice blends.

Many Asian and Indian dishes use Guntur Sannam chili peppers as a flavoring. They are also commonly used as a condiment, being diced and crushed into hot sauces or salsa, and they can also be cut into thin slices and added to rice for flavoring.

HABANERO

Pronunciation: ah-bah-NAIR-oh
Length: 1 - 2 ½"
Width: 1 - 2"
Scientific Name: Capsicum chinense
Other Names: black habanero is a name given to dark brown habaneros that have an exotic and unusual taste.
Scoville Range: 100,000 - 350,000

Origin and History

The habanero originated in Cuba and the name means "from Havana." Cubans introduced habanero peppers to Mexico's Yucatan Peninsula, from which Spaniards distributed it to warm climates around the world. Mistakenly believing the plant was from China, early taxonomists called it Capsicum chinense.

The Yucatan Peninsula is by far the most major area of cultivation for the habanero, with 1,500 tons harvested each year. Mexico is the largest consumer of habaneros as this fiery pepper is central to Yucatan cuisine. Habaneros are also grown in Belize, Costa Rica, Texas, and California, but to a much lesser extent.

Description

Intensely spicy habanero peppers are among the hottest of the chile peppers. The fruity, citrus-like flavor has a floral aroma and the flesh is thin and waxy.

Habanero peppers are round, oblong, or lantern shaped. The unripe green fruits change to red or orange (or, less commonly, brown, white, or pink) as they mature.

Each compact, attractive, upright bush can sport dozens of peppers. The chiles can be dried and ground for pepper flakes and Mexican and oriental food stores often carry fresh pods.

Scotch bonnet, so named after its shape, has the same type of flesh, heat level, and flavor as the standard habanero, but with a different pod size and shape. It is more heavily cultivated in Caribbean countries.

How to Serve or Use

Habanero peppers are used to make foods hot and spicy. They are typically used dried, pickled, or fresh in salsas and salads. Dried habaneros, which remain viable for long periods of time, can be reconstituted in sauce mixes by adding water. Habanero jelly is a spicy accompaniment to grilled meats and fish.

Habanero chile is added to tequila or mescal to make spicy versions of these drinks. Small slivers of black habaneros add extra fiery heat and exotic taste. Extracts of habanero are so hot only a drop or two are added to sauces. In fact, habaneros are so hot that some bottled sauces carry labels warning consumers to wash their hands after contact and avoid getting the sauce in the eyes.

HUNGARIAN YELLOW WAX

Pronunciation: hung-GAR-e-an
Length: 6 - 8"
Width: 1 ½"
Scientific Name: Capsicum annum
Other Names: hot yellow pepper, hot wax pepper
Scoville Range: 5,000 - 15,000

Origin and History

Hungarian yellow wax peppers were first developed in Hungary and other parts of Europe. They are called yellow wax peppers because of their pastel yellow bees' wax color in addition to the sheen and texture of the skin.

Hungarian yellow wax peppers start growing best in temperatures between 64° and 90° and take around 65 days to mature. The peppers start green and then turn to yellow when they are normally harvested. If left to fully ripen they turn red in color and their heat intensifies while they remain sweet.

Description

The Hungarian wax is a large pepper that tapers to a rounded point and has thin, translucent skin. The waxy skin is flavorful and does not need to be peeled. The pepper has a medium to mild heat.

While the Hungarian wax is closely related to the mild banana pepper, it is an entirely different fruit. It can easily be mistaken for the banana chile because they look the same. The difference in taste is what distinguishes the two since the Hungarian yellow wax is much hotter than the mild banana pepper.

How to Serve or Use

Hungarian wax peppers are used in soups and stews. Their large size makes them ideal for pickling to serve as appetizers. They can be stuffed with different ingredients such as meat and rice. They are served fresh in salads and salsas to add color and a spicy flavor. Some recipes call for roasting or grilling the peppers before adding them to intensify the flavor.

Hungarian yellow wax peppers can be purchased at grocery stores or specialty markets. They should be wrapped in paper and kept refrigerated and can be stored for about one week.

JALAPENO

Pronunciation: Ha-lay-pay-ne-oh
Length: 2 - 3 ½"
Width: less than 1"
Scientific Name: Capsicum annuum
Other Names: huachinango, jalapimento, chile gordo
Scoville Range: 2,500 - 8,000

Origin and History

The jalapeno pepper originated in Mexico and derives its name from the town of Xalapa, Veracruz, where it was traditionally cultivated. One of the largest places to grow jalapeno peppers is in Papaloapan, Mexico, which is a river basin north of Veracruz.

In the United States, jalapeno peppers are grown predominantly in southern New Mexico and western Texas and the jalapeno is the state pepper of Texas. They are the most commonly used pepper in the United States and can be found in almost any grocery store.

Description

The jalapeno pepper is considered a pod pepper, and is about 2 to 3 ½ inches long. Its narrow girth and uneven skin contour give it its unique shape and texture. The growing period lasts between 70 to 80 days and when fully mature the jalapeno plant will stand about 3 feet tall.

Although most jalapeno peppers are green when they are picked, they will continue to ripen and turn red if not used shortly after harvesting. A good jalapeno pepper should be firm and smooth skinned and have a solid green coloring. Dry lines in the ridge of the pepper indicate a more mature and hotter pepper.

How to Serve or Use

Jalapeno peppers are a versatile pepper and can be used in a variety of different ways. They can be sauteed in oil and served with melted cheese on top, smoked and used in a variety of rice dishes, or they can be ground up or muddled and served in mixed drinks.

Jalapenos are a favorite in many Mexican dishes, salads, and sauces. They are used in many Tex-Mex dishes as well such as jalapeno poppers, nachos, and burritos. They are also commonly made into jalapeno jelly or pickled. And when smoked and dried they become the chipotle pepper.

Kashmiri

Pronunciation: Ka-jsh-me-er-ee
Length: 2"
Width: 1"
Scientific Name: Capsicum annuum
Other Names: byadgi
Scoville Range: 2,500 - 5,000

Origin and History

The true origin of the Kashmiri pepper is from the northern most region of India, in the war torn region known as Kashmiri. However, there are not enough Kashmiri peppers produced to keep up with the growing demand and there have been a number of imitation peppers that have emerged throughout the years. The most popular is the Byadgi chile, named after the Indian town.

The Kashmiri pepper has a bright crimson color, which when used in cooking turns the other food in a dish red. Many imitation or mock Kashmiri chilies do not possess this intense crimson color.

Description

A genuine Kashmiri pepper will have a robust crimson coloring and smooth and shiny skin. When dried the skin becomes even smoother and shinier.

The Kashmiri pepper also has a fruity flavor, which adds robustness to any meal. It has also been compared to paprika but with more heat.

How to Serve or Use

Kashmiri chiles are traditionally used in Indian dishes to add mild spice and the deep red color. They are usually a main component of Rogan Josh, an aromatic North Indian mutton curry, and Rista, a meatball dish, both from Kashmiri.

Kashmiri peppers are almost exclusively used dried. It can be hard to find whole dried peppers in North America but you can often find Kashmiri powder. The powder can be used to flavor anything from curries or chutneys to BBQ rubs.

KOREAN

Pronunciation: kor-RE-an
Length: 4 - 5"
Width: ½"
Scientific Name: Capsicum annuum
Other Names: inchanga chile, kochu
Scoville Range: 50,000 - 100,000

Origin and History

The Korean chile was reluctantly introduced to the Koreans by the Japanese in the 17th century. It was called the "Japanese mustard" by Portuguese missionaries. It was once believed that the chile would grow only in its native regions of Central and South America but today there are over 1 million kg exported from Korea each year.

Before the chile was introduced, Korean cuisine did not contain red pepper. At that time, dishes were flavored with salt and alcohol. At present, it is reported that Koreans consume the highest chile per capita in the world. The chile is popular not only for the taste but its nutrients which include protein, carotene and vitamin B12.

Description

The chile goes from a dark green to bright red at maturity, which takes 90 to 100 days. The pepper has a thin wall and tapered, elongated shape with glossy skin and the shell contains a large number of seeds.

The flavor of the Korean chile is very distinct because of the unique geography of Korean's mountainous regions, sea air, soil and water. Its pungency makes it well suited for chile powder.

How to Serve or Use

Korean chiles are used fully ripe, dried, powdered and as a paste. Korean chile paste is also known as kochu-jang or gochujang. It is used in stews, soups and as a marinade. The paste makes a spicy vegetable dip and is also prepared as a broth by adding boiling water. The chile paste has several medicinal benefits which include helping blood circulation and aiding in weight loss.

Korean chile pepper flavors kim chi, or pickled vegetables, which is an important dish in the Korean diet. It is used as an ingredient in several spicy stuffing recipes. Korean chiles are also added to pan fried pork slices for extra essence. Cucumbers sprinkled with Korean chile are an easy to prepare appetizer.

Malagueta

Length: 1 - 2"
Width: ½"
Scientific Name: Capsicum frutescens var. malagueta
Other Names: malaguentinha, piri-piri, malaguetao, malagueto, malaguetta
Scoville Range: 60,000 - 100,000

Origin and History

The malagueta chile is widely used in Brazil, Mozambique, and Portugal. It is often confused with the unrelated melegueta pepper, a spice from West Africa. The confusion stems from when the Brazilian state of Bahia was a center of the slave trade. Apparently, slaves brought from Africa called the native Brazilian pepper by the Portuguese name for the West African spice.

The malagueta chile is one of the most widely used hot peppers in Brazil.

Description

The appearance and flavor of the small, tapered malagueta chile are similar to those of the pungent bird's eye or Thai chile. These searing hot red peppers have wrinkly skin. Markets typically carry two sizes, which are simply the same chile picked at different stages of growth. Locals may call the two sizes by different names. The smaller ones are "malaguetinha" in Brazil and "piri-piri" in Portugal and Mozambique. Brazilians call the larger ones "malaguetao," while the Portuguese call them "malagueta."

How to Serve or Use

Malagueta chiles can be used in a number of different ways, and at different stages of ripeness. They can be minced with oil, added to salsa, served as a table condiment, made into hot sauce, or used in recipes to season dishes.

Malagueta chiles make a spicy sauce for meat and fish. The malagueta chile is an ingredient in many regional dishes of Mozambique and Brazil, particularly xinxim, acaraje, and other Bahian street food. This street food is typically sold by women who wear white cotton dresses and colorful caps and headscarves. In Portugal, malagueta chiles are mainly cooked with poultry.

Recipes that use malagueta chiles include, among many others:

- Malagueta pepper, tomato, and coconut sauce
- Brazilian fish stew
- Malagueta chile sauce
- Malagueta pepper oil
- Mussels and sausage with malagueta pepper
- Roasted rack of lamb with malagueta pepper
- Piri piri prawns.

Manzano

Pronunciation: Mahn-zah-noh
Length: 2 - 3"
Width: 2 - 3"
Scientific Name: Capsicum pubescens
Other Names: peron, caballo, ciruelo, rocoto
Scoville Range: 10,000 - 30,000

Origin and History

The manzano pepper is one of the only chili peppers that is cultivated and grown in Mexico that is not included in the capsicum annuum family. It comes from the capsicum pubescens, which are indigenous to the Andes mountain range region of Chile and Argentina, and also parts of Bolivia. It is closely related to the rocoto pepper from South America.

The name manzano can be directly translated into English as "apple" because its appearance and shape resembles a small apple. In some parts of the Americas they are commonly referred to as "el mas picante de los picantes," the hottest of the hot.

It is commonly grown in the high elevations in the Mexican states of Chiapas, Queretaro, and Guerrero. The manzano pepper is especially resilient to cold temperatures, which makes it ideal for its mountainous locale.

Description

The manzano plant generally grows at high altitudes and is a rugged shrub that produces a yellow-orange pepper when it reaches maturity. What makes the manzano pepper unique compared to other peppers throughout the world is that its seeds are black.

Manzano peppers are spherical and turn a bright yellow, orange, or red when ripe. They also have thick skin which makes them difficult to dry.

How to Serve or Use

Because of the manzano pepper's thick, fleshy skin it is an ideal pepper for use in hot salsas. The skin also makes them hard to dry and they are almost always used fresh.

Manzano peppers are also commonly stuffed with meat or cheese and baked.

Manzano peppers are commonly used to make a spicy Huacatay sauce, a Peruvian sauce.

Mirasol

Length: 3 - 5"
Width: ¾"
Scientific Name: Capsicum annuum
Other Names: chile trompa, casabel, guajillo
Scoville Range: 2,500 - 5,000

Origin and History

The Spanish word mirasol means "looking at the sun." The pepper was given this name because it grows in an upward direction on the plant. Mirasol peppers are grown on more than 40,000 acres of land in Mexico. The pepper is used in Mexican as well as Peruvian cuisine.

Description

Mirasol chile peppers come in more varieties than any other chile. This variance makes them hard to recognize. The pepper varies in size and texture; it is sometimes smooth and other times wrinkled. Mirasol plants grow 18 to 24 inches in full sun and ripen in 80 to 90 days. The peppers turn from green to bright orange-red when they are ripe. Mirasol peppers have a thin skin and are slightly curved.

The mirasol chile has a unique spicy flavor that is compared to berries and other fruit. The medium heat is direct and intense yet very flavorful.

How to Serve or Use

Mirasol chiles are used in soups stews and sauces. It is also used to flavor potatoes, pork and chicken. Tacos, quesadillas and Mexican salads commonly contain mirasol peppers. Mirasol peppers have also made their way into nontraditional dishes such as macaroni and cheese and chocolate cake.

Mirasol chile is used fresh or in dried, powder, and paste form. Homemade paste can be made by soaking the dried chiles in water over a six hour period with two changes of water. The chiles are washed under water, including rubbing the peppers together to clean the inner side. After they are cut the chiles are boiled for two hours, changing the water two times to remove the heat. They are then blended with vegetable oil to give them the paste consistency.

Mulato

Pronunciation: moo-LAH-toe
Length: 4 - 6"
Width: 2 ½"
Scientific Name: Capsicum annuum
Other Names: mulatto chile
Scoville Range: 2,500 - 3,000

Origin and History

Originating in Mexico, the mulato chile is closely related to the poblano and the ancho chiles. Ancho and mulato chiles may be cultivars of the poblano, or the differences may be regional. The relationship between the three chiles remains unclear.

Mole, a sauce that often includes mulato chiles, originated in the Mexican states of Puebla, Oaxaco, and/or Tiaxcala.

Description

The mulato chile has a heat that ranges from mild to medium. The dark green pods mature to a rich red or brown color. Dried, the pods are flat, deeply wrinkled, and brownish black. Pods are wide at the top, tapering to a blunt point and are somewhat pear shaped.

The vigorous plants reach 18 to 24 inches tall and typically have high yields. The plants have green stems, green leaves, and white flowers.

The distinctive biting taste of the mulato chile is like licorice or chocolate with undertones of cherry and tobacco. With its light fruity nuance, the mulato chile is sweeter than the ancho chile.

How to Serve or Use

Mulato chile is mostly sold dry. Dried mulato chiles can be reconstituted in boiling water or ground into chili powder. They add a rich flavor and mild heat to soups, salsa, and sauces, and are even used in desserts.

Along with ancho and pasilla chiles, mulato is a common ingredient in mole poblano, the dark brown spicy/chocolaty sauce typically served over meat or poultry. Dried mulato chiles are ideal for many mole recipes because they keep their dark brown color after soaking.

The mulato chile is also an ingredient in many other Mexican sauces and stews, including chicken with rice. Mexican cooks make stuffed mulato peppers by rehydrating the pods; trimming out the seed cores; stuffing the pods with shrimp, cheese, and breadcrumbs; and pan frying the stuffed peppers in oil.

Dried mulato chiles will retain their potency for a year or more if stored in an air-tight container in a cool and dark location. To reconstitute, soak the dried chiles in boiling water for 15 minutes.

NAGA JOLOKIA

Pronunciation: Nah-gah Jo-Loh-kee-ah
Length: 2 - 4"
Width: 1"
Scientific Name: Capsicum chinense
Other Names: bhut jolokia
Scoville Range: 850,000 - 1,000,000

Origin and History

Welcome to the world's hottest chili pepper, according to many people. The Naga Jolokia pepper is believed to have originated in the Assam region of northeast India. It is actually a hybrid pepper, combining peppers from regions of India and Bangladesh and was originally called "Bhot," for the Bhotiya region, or "Naga," for the Nagaland hills, both believed to be places of origin for the pepper. "Jolokia" is simply the Assamese word for the Capsicum pepper. It has been called the "ghost pepper" by members of the United States media because a claim that "bhut" means ghost, which has been refuted by the Indian researchers from Nagaland University.

This pepper grows in the Indian states of Nagaland, Manipur, and Assam, as well as the Sylhet region of Bangladesh. This interspecific species of pepper belongs predominantly to the capsicum chinense family, but also contains some genetic markers of the capsicum frutescens.

The Guinness World Records certified the Naga Jolokia as the hottest chili pepper in the world. This lasted until 2010 when it was replaced by the Naga Viper, whose "average peak" is more than 300,000 points higher than an average Naga Jolokia. Then in February 2011 the Infinity chili took the record. Of course, the exact hotness of peppers is very controversial and proponents for all three peppers argue about which one is truly the hottest.

Description

Like most chili peppers, the Naga Jolokia pepper is initially light green then ripens to orange or red. The redder and riper the pepper, the hotter it is. The pepper plant itself grows about 3 feet tall and can produce over 100 peppers in its lifetime. Since the Naga Jolokia hasn't been selectively breed it results in a lot of variety in plant and pepper size, as well at hotness.

Bhut Jolokia have a very characteristic claw shape and rough, uneven skin which is pretty unique among peppers. The skin is also very thin.

How to Serve or Use

As a food, the Naga Jolokia has limited uses besides adding pure heat to dishes. With its extreme heat a little goes a long way in food. It's commonly made into hot sauces where one dash is all that is needed to season a meal.

The Naga Jolokia is often used to help relieve stomach aches and indigestion through traditional homeopathic remedies. They are also used in smoke bombs or smeared on fences to keep out wild elephants, and would presumably do the same for deer or moose.

India's Defense Research and Development Organization is working on ways to incorporate it into various non-lethal weapons such as smoke grenades and pepper spray.

NAGA VIPER

Length: 1 - 2 ½"
Width: 1 - 2"
Scientific Name: Capsicum hybrid
Scoville Range: 855,000 - 1,359,000

Origin and History

Naga Viper is poised to officially become the hottest pepper in the world. Gerald Fowler of the Chili Pepper House bred Naga Viper in a greenhouse in Cumbria, England. To do that he crossed three of the hottest known peppers: Bhut Joloika, Naga Morichi and Trinidad Scorpion.

Naga Viper tested hotter than Bhut Jolokia, the reigning champion. In December 2010, Warwick University testing labs confirmed Naga Viper as the world's hottest chili pepper, guaranteeing it a spot in the next edition of the Guinness Book of World Records. To put it in perspective, Naga Viper is 270 times hotter than a jalapeno pepper, "hot enough to strip paint." "Naga" means "Cobra Snake" in Sanskrit.

The triumph of Naga Viper may be challenged, however. Critics claim the hybrid is unstable and cannot be reproduced and its heat rating is unreliable.

Description

Naga Viper is described as having a blistering heat without the unpleasant taste or smell or some other extremely hot peppers. The flavor is described as fruity, spicy, and hot. The ripe pod is red, plump, and wrinkly, tapering to a sharp point. The fruit feels crunchy and warm in the mouth.

Mr. Fowler says of his fiery creation, "It numbs your tongue, then burns all the way down. It can last an hour, and you just don't want to talk to anyone or do anything. But it's a marvelous endorphin rush. It makes you feel great."

How to Serve or Use

Naga Viper is used to make an extremely hot sauce called "The Terminator." It must be used with extreme caution; a drop is enough to heat up a dish. The few people who have eaten Naga Viper peppers report burning throats, tearing eyes, and heavy breathing.

The Indian government is reportedly exploring ways to use the hottest peppers like Bhut Jolokia and Naga Viper to create spice bombs that could incapacitate enemy soldiers without killing them. Mr. Fowler has made seeds of Naga Viper available to growers in Afghanistan as a replacement for the heroin poppy.

NEW MEXICO

Pronunciation: noo-MEK-sih-koe
Length: 6 - 8"
Width: 2"
Scientific Name: Capsicum annuum
Scoville Range: 1,000 - 1,500

Origin and History

In 1958 New Mexico State University released a pepper called New Mexico No. 6. New Mexico 6-4 is a less hot version of that variety. One of the New Mexican-type chiles (also referred to as "long green" or "Anaheim" types); New Mexico 6-4 has increased yield and improved quality as a result of scientific breeding.

New Mexico has more land in chile pepper cultivation than any other state in the U.S. New Mexico 6-4 is an important crop in the state's extensive chile industry.

Description

New Mexico 6-4 has large tapered pods with rounded shoulders and blunt tips. Pods have thick, smooth flesh, and change from green to red as they mature. Harvest occurs when the fruit turns red.

The plants grow 18 to 24 inches high. The heat level is mild to medium and the flavor is slightly sweet.

New Mexico 6-4 is the standard pepper used by commercial chile processors. It is readily available in restaurants and markets. This mild cultivar is used as both a red and a green chile.

How to Serve or Use

Most of the New Mexico 6-4 red chiles are dried and crushed to make flakes or powder, which have a variety of culinary uses.

Both the green and the red fruit are excellent in soups and stews. They are used in Mexican and New Mexican dishes such as chili, enchiladas, and green chile stew. They are ideal for making chile rellenos - chiles stuffed with cheese, coated in egg, and fried.

New Mexico 6-4 takes well to roasting. To roast, remove the seeds and sear the fruit over a gas flame or in the broiler until the skin blackens then put them in a plastic bag to cool and then remove the skin. New Mexico 6-4 freezes and cans well and is good for eating fresh. Chili powder is made from the dried ripe red chiles.

New Mexico 6-4 pods are among the easiest pods to use to make rista, the long strings of chiles seen in the southwest.

Pasilla

Pronunciation: pah-SEE-yah
Length: 6 - 8"
Width: 1 - 1 ½"
Scientific Name: Capsicum annuum
Other Names: chile negro, chilaca, mexican negro
Scoville Range: 1,000 - 2,000

Origin and History

The pasilla pepper originated south of Mexico City in the Puebla region of Mexico. Pasilla literally means "little raisin" and was named for its dark wrinkled skin and raisin aroma. It is a dried form of the chilaca pepper, a very common Mexican chile used in a variety of dishes. Combined with ancho and mulato chiles it is a very common ingredient in mole. Pasilla is often mistaken for the ancho, which is a dried poblano chile.

Description

Pasilla is a long, shiny pepper with a dark green color. It gradually darkens until it turns to colors ranging from dark brown to black at full maturity. The pepper is easily available in the US, Mexico, and the UK in both dried and powdered form. The taste of the chile is rich and smoky and the heat is mild to medium.

Pasilla chiles are rich in minerals like iron, niacin, and magnesium. They also contain vitamins B1, B2 and D. One pasilla pepper provides close to the total amount of Vitamin C needed daily for adults. The pasilla chile is low in calories and sodium. It is cholesterol free and fat free with high fiber content.

How to Serve or Use

Pasillas are always cooked or roasted before using. It is frequently added to soups, sauces and stews. One easy way to prepare stew is made from diced pasillas, potatoes and onions cooked in chicken stock until tender. Pasillas pair especially well with duck and lamb. Mushrooms, garlic, honey and oregano are among other flavors that are compatible with the pasilla chile.

Leftover chicken can be used to make stuffed pasilla peppers and served with salad for a quick meal. Pork, rice and cheese are also ingredients used to make stuffing for pasilla chiles. Battered and fried pasilla peppers are served as appetizers. The peppers can be used to make a Cajun seasoning when blended with other chiles and herbs like oregano and sage. Crepes filled with a puree of roasted pasilla peppers, onions, cheese and shiitake mushrooms are often served in restaurants.

Boiling the peppers in water for about 10 minutes before adding to a dish releases their full flavor. Although they are not especially hot, hands should be kept away from the eyes and washed thoroughly when handling pasillas to avoid irritation or burning. Dried peppers stay fresh for 1 to 2 two weeks when they are stored in a cool and dry area.

Pequin

Pronunciation: pee/puh-KEEN
Length: ¾"
Width: ¼"
Scientific Name: Capsicum annuum
Other Names: chile petin, chile piquin, bird pepper, turkey pepper, cayenne pepper, chile de monte
Scoville Range: 100,000 - 400,000

Origin and History

Anthropologists have traced the chile pequin back 7,000 years to Bolivia and Brazil. Some believe it to be the original wild pepper, the mother of all peppers. It is still found in the wild in South America, Latin America, and the southern United States, most notably south Texas. Chile pequin grows under cultivation in Texas and Mexico. Birds generously spread the seeds.

Description

The tiniest of chiles ("pequin" means "small"), the chile pequin is round or oval, changing from green to brilliant red or reddish orange as it matures, eventually turning brown. Chile pequin grows on compact plants that are 1 to 3 feet tall. The complex flavor of this extremely hot chile is at once citrusy, smoky, sweet, and nutty.

Depending on the climate and growing conditions, chile pequins may ripen throughout the year. Harvesting is by hand without damaging the plant or by cutting down branches and then removing the fruit. Commercially grown plants may produce as much as two pounds of chiles per plant.

How to Serve or Use

While many different dishes and cuisines use chile pequin, it is particularly common in Mexican and Southeast Asian cooking. The green fruits may be pickled or added fresh to salsa, while the red ones are dried. Drying makes the chiles last longer and gives them a more focused flavor. Fresh chiles stay fresh for about one week in a plastic bag in the refrigerator. Dried pequin chiles will remain potent for at least a year if stored in an air-tight container in a dark, cool location.

The most common use of pequin chiles is in liquid hot pepper seasoning. Cooks use pequins in soups, vinegars, salsas, and salads. With capers and garlic they go well with fish. Dried chile pequins are mixed with lemon and salt and sprinkled on mangoes or pineapple.

Rehydrated dried pequin chiles are added to soups and sauces. Alternatively, the dried chiles can be toasted slightly and added to dishes without rehydrating. Dried chile pequins can also be ground into chili powder.

Two or three crushed tiny peppers are enough to heat up a whole pot of soup or a bowl of beans. Small but powerful, this pepper has a fiery taste that is well suited to ultra spicy dishes.

POBLANO

Pronunciation: puh-blah-noh; Sp. paw-blah-naw
Length: 3 - 6"
Width: 2 - 3"
Scientific Name: Capsicum annuum
Other Names: pablano
Scoville Range: 1,000 - 1,500

Origin and History

The poblano pepper originally comes from the State of Puebla, Mexico and "Poblano" is also the word for an inhabitant of that region. It is one of the most popular peppers in Mexico and is rather mild. Poblanos have also become popular in the United States and can be found in many grocery stores in the states bordering Mexico and in urban areas across the country.

One reason for the poblano's popularity is its use in Chiles en Nogada, a traditional dish served during the Mexican independence festivals. The dish uses green, white, and red ingredients to symbolize the Mexican flag and is considered one of the most symbolic dishes in Mexico.

Description

Poblanos tend to be among the mildest of peppers but occasionally a pepper can be very hot. The heat of poblanos can even vary substantially on the same plant. The mild peppers generally taste like a bell pepper with a little bit of peppery heat.

The poblano plant is about 2 feet tall and has many stems that become loaded with peppers about 3 to 6 inches long and 2 to 3 inches wide that taper towards the bottom. A young, unripe poblano pepper is a dark purplish green but as it ripens it turns into a very deep and dark red that can appear black. They are good to eat as soon as they start to turn red (or just before) and last until they start to become wrinkled and soft.

When dried, the poblano is called an ancho pepper and takes on fruity, musky flavor. Ancho peppers are often ground into powder for flavoring. The poblano is also closely related to the mulato, which is darker in color, sweeter in flavor and softer in texture and is often dried as well. Poblanos are also often mislabeled as pasilla peppers.

How to Serve or Use

Poblanos are used in many dishes besides Chiles en Nogada. They can be coated with whipped egg and fried to make capeado. Poblanos are often stuffed for the popular dish of Chile relleno. Poblanos are also commonly used in mole sauces, especially Mole Poblano which is the spicy chocolate chili sauce originating in Puebla.

Often times the fresh poblanos are charred or roasted and the skin, membrane and seeds are removed. The charring also sweetens the flesh and adds a light smokiness. At this point, poblanos can also be canned or frozen.

RED SAVINA HABANERO

Length: 1 ½ - 2 ½"
Width: 1 - 1 ½"
Scientific Name: Capsicum chinense
jacq. var. red savina
Other Names: dominican devil's tongue, ball of fire
Scoville Range: 350,000 - 580,000

Origin and History

Red Savina is a cultivar of habanero pepper, bred by GNS Spices in Walnut, California. Frank Garcia, one of the owners of GNS Spices, found a plant with red pods in his field of orange-podded plants. He grew the seeds, and from the seedlings he selectively bred a plant that produces hotter, heavier, and larger pods. He called the cultivar Red Savina habanero.

"Red Savina" is a trademark owned by GNS Spices. It can only be grown commercially under license from that company. It is the first habanero to receive plant protection certification from the U.S. Department of Agriculture.

The Guinness Book of World Records lists Red Savina as the hottest habanero pepper in the world. Red Savina held the record as the hottest of all chile peppers from 1994 until 2006, when the twice-as-hot Naga Jolokia pepper overtook it.

Description

This extremely hot, bright red pepper has wrinkled skin. The tapered pods hang on plants that reach 2 to 3 ½ feet tall. Each plant produces up to 50 pods.

Red Savina is twice as hot as the regular habanero and 65 times hotter than a jalapeno pepper. One gram is enough to heat up over 1,200 pounds of sauce. It takes over eight pounds of fresh fruit to make one pound of the dried spice.

How to Serve or Use

Red Savina is sold as bottled pepper powder, sauce, and extract. Dried and smoked whole chile pods are available. People eat the fiery dried or fresh peppers at their own risk. Added to dark chocolate, it makes a special treat.

Even without eating, Red Savina is a hazard; it can cause blisters on sensitive skin. It is so hot and potentially dangerous that some retailers will not sell pure Red Savina to minors!

Red Savina is also an ingredient in the hot pepper sprays police use to control crowds.

Rocotillo

Length: 1"
Width: 1 ½"
Scientific Name: Capsicum baccatum and Capsicum chinense
Other Names: squash pepper
Scoville Range: 1,500 - 2,500

Origin and History

Confusion surrounds the origin and naming of the rocotillo chile. Rocotillo chiles appear to be varieties of both Capsicum baccatum and Capsicum chinense. While they have similar appearance and heat, their origins differ. The baccatum variety is from Peru, but the exact origin of the chinense version is not known for certain. In addition, different hot peppers are called rocotillo in different parts of Central and South America.

Cuba and Puerto Rico also grow rocotillo chiles, as does Texas and other warm U.S. states.

Description

The small, brilliant red peppers have a fruity taste with a mild to medium heat described as hot enough to be interesting, but not biting. Short and wide, the thin-fleshed peppers have an unusual shape that is similar to the patty pan squash, hence the nickname "squash pepper."

The unripe fruit are green or yellow and they mature to red or (less commonly) orange or brown. They are harvested and used in both the ripe and unripe states. Markets carry the fresh pods seasonally.

Rocotillo chiles grow on plants that are 2 to 3 feet tall and 1 to 3 feet wide. The fruit grow in clusters of 2 to 4 pods. The bushy plants are compact and very productive.

How to Serve or Use

Rocotillo chiles dry easily. They are popular in Spanish dishes, including soups and stews, and are also eaten fresh.

Rocotillos are used in salsa (e.g. rocotillo-mango relish and Spanish-Caribbean Salsa), as a garnish for beans, and roasted with beef or lamb. Rocotillo pepper and pasta salad with white vinegar and black olives makes good use of this relatively mild pepper. A recipe for rice pilaf with shrimp uses rocotillo chile for its flavor and moderate heat.

Rocotillo chiles work well sauted by themselves or with other vegetables. In beans or in the traditional carne asada (thinly sliced marinated and grilled beef); rocotillo chiles are served as an accompanying condiment or cooked with the food.

Fresh, unwashed peppers store well in the refrigerator in a plastic bag for one week.

SANTAKA

Pronunciation: San-tah-ka
Length: 2 - 2 ½"
Width: Less than 1"
Scientific Name: Capsicum annuum
Other Names: none
Scoville Range: 40,000 - 50,000

Origin and History

The santaka pepper plant originates in Asia and is commonly used in a host of Asian dishes. It is a hearty and robust plant that can endure in a range of climate conditions which makes it ideal for a number of pepper enthusiasts. The average plant can produce up to 150 peppers in its lifetime.

Description

The peppers grow on 2 to 3 foot plants that produce white flowers. The peppers grow upwards out of the flowers and are red and green. The maturation process takes about 80 days. The peppers have thin flesh and an intense spicy flavor.

The santaka pepper plant is an aesthetically pleasing plant and many people plant them in their garden for show. They allow the peppers to fall from the plant after ripening and till them into the soil.

How to Serve or Use

The santaka pepper is widely used to add heat and flavor in many Asian cuisines. They are often thinly sliced and added to stir fries for heat. They can also be used for salsas and of course hot sauces.

SCOTCH BONNET

Pronunciation: skoch-BON-net
Length: 1 ½"
Width: 1 - 1 ½"
Scientific Name: Capsicum chinense
Other Names: boabs bonnet, scotty bons, jamaican pepper, martinique pepper
Scoville Range: 100,000 - 350,000

Origin and History

Scotch bonnet peppers are mainly found in Caribbean and Maldives Islands. The pepper is popular in Jamaican, Grenadian, Haitian and Trinidadian cuisine. The name scotch bonnet refers to its shape which resembles a Scottish men's bonnet, later adopted by women, known as a "tam." The pepper originates from the same species as the habanero pepper. It is sometimes labeled "hot pepper" or "big pepper" in markets.

The scotch bonnet is easy to grow and requires little attention. The peppers thrive in a long, hot growing season like tomatoes. They are grown in greenhouses in areas with inconsistent heat and sun. If the plant is kept warm, watered and fed once a week it should produce an abundance of peppers.

Description

Scotch bonnets are small peppers that are irregular in shape. Ripe peppers change colors from green through various shades of orange and red. They are known as one of the hottest peppers in the world. Beyond the intense heat, the flavor of the pepper is earthy and slightly sweet. The fruity taste has been described as being close to the flavor of apricots.

How to Serve or Use

This very hot pepper can be purchased from markets and specialty stores. It is available fresh and in dried form. For cooks who are brave enough to cook with the pepper, the seeds must be removed before it is added to the dish. The seeds can be reserved for planting. In some recipes the pepper is chopped or diced and added to the dish when it first begins cooking. Other cooks use the pepper whole to add heat to the dish and remove it when the dish is finished cooking.

The most well-known use of scotch bonnet peppers is in traditional Jamaican jerk seasoning. It is combined with allspice and several other spices to create the distinct jerk spice mix.

Another common use for scotch bonnet peppers is a West Indian pepper sauce. This condiment is used to spice up poultry, fish and meat. Scotch bonnet can be a seasoning for soups and stews. They are also used to make marinades and barbeque sauces, where they provide a flavorful balance to fruits such as mango.

Serrano

Pronunciation: seh-RAH-noe
Length: 2 ¼"
Width: ½"
Scientific Name: Capsicum annuum
Other Names: chili seco
Scoville Range: 10,000 - 25,000

Origin and History

The serrano pepper originated in the mountainous regions of the Mexican states of Hidalgo and Puebla. The name "serrano" refers to the mountains ("sierras") of these regions.

The Mexican states of Veracruz, Tamaulipas, Nayarit, and Sinaloa are the major producers of serrano chiles.

Description

Serrano peppers may be the hottest chile that is commonly available in the U.S. They are sold in specialty markets and most grocery stores.

Serrano pepper plants are 1 ½ to 5 feet tall with up to 50 hanging pods per plant. Shaped like elongated cylinders or candle flames, serrano chiles have a blunt end, thin walls, and thick flesh. The unripe peppers are green while mature colors vary, including green, red, brown, orange, and yellow. The savory and spicy flavor is crisp, full-bodied, and biting. While they look similar to the jalapeno, serranos are smaller and much hotter but with a less harsh bite.

Fresh serrano peppers have smooth, firm skin with solid coloring and medium-thick flesh. Peppers with soft, bruised, or wrinkled skin are past their prime.

How to Serve or Use

Serrano chiles add bold, uncomplicated heat to recipes. They are used in salsas and sauces and are eaten raw.

Serrano chiles are typically eaten raw in southwestern and Mexican cuisine. They are used in making pico de gallo, which is a fresh, uncooked salsa made from chopped tomato, onion and chiles. Because of their fleshy walls they do not need to be steamed or peeled before using, but some salsa recipes call for roasting them. Serrano peppers can also be pickled, creating a dish called sport peppers. Some pepper aficionados consider serranos too meaty to dry well, while others report sprinkling dried serrano chiles on top of a margarita for a unique and fiery drink.

Smoking dried serrano chiles deepens the flavor. The dried peppers can be ground into chili powder or reconstituted before using. To reconstitute the dried peppers, soak them in boiling water for 15 minutes.

TABASCO

Pronunciation: tuh-bas-koh
Length: 1 ½ - 2"
Width: 2"
Scientific Name: Capsicum frutescens,
Other Names: Tabasco pimienta, chile pepper
Scoville Range: 30,000 - 50,000

ORIGIN AND HISTORY

This chile is named after the state of Tabasco in the southeast region of Mexico where it was originally grown. In 1848 the peppers were moved to Louisiana and used to make the popular hot sauce. Most Tabasco pepper crop is grown in Central and South America and moved to Louisiana to be manufactured.

To determine if they are ready to be picked a small red stick is placed against Tabasco chiles to check for proper color. The weight and juiciness of the chile also determines if it is ripe. Tabasco chiles are harvested by hand and are difficult to pick.

In the 1960's Tabasco peppers were infected by the tobacco mosaic virus, an infectious disease found in tobacco plants. In 1970 the Greenleaf Tabasco was introduced as the first resistant Tabasco crop to be cultivated.

DESCRIPTION

A Tabasco bush can grow up to 5 feet tall. The tapered chiles grow upward on their stems and have a smooth skin. The pepper starts as soft yellow to red and matures to yellow and orange until turning a bright red when it is fully ripe.

Tabasco is the only variety of chile pepper that is juicy, not dry, on the inside. It is a very pungent chile with a hot, sometimes bitter taste.

HOW TO SERVE OR USE

Tabasco chile is the main ingredient in the hot sauce with the same name. The sauce is a condiment used to flavor fish, meat, eggs and other food. Tabasco sauce is often used to spice up Bloody Mary cocktails. Peppered vinegar can also be flavored with Tabasco chile.

Tabasco peppers are found fresh and in a dried powder. Fresh peppers can be added to vinegar to make a spicy vinegar sauce. The chile is also pickled and made into hot pepper jelly.

Tabasco pepper sauce has been included with U.S. military Meals, Ready to Eat (MRE's) since the 1980's. It is also on the menu of the NASA space shuttle program, Skylab and the International Space Station.

Thai

Pronunciation: tahy
Length: ½ - 1 ½"
Width: ¼ - ½"
Scientific Name: Capsicum frutescens
Other Names: bird's eye chili, chili padi, cili padi, boonie pepper
Scoville Range: 50,000 - 100,000

Origin and History

Like most hot peppers, Thai pepper originated in Central and South America and was spread by the Spanish and Portuguese to Southeast Asia and other tropical and subtropical regions. It now grows wild in addition to being cultivated in Thailand, Malaysia, Indonesia, Cambodia, Vietnam, Laos, the Philippines, India, and Singapore.

Description

Small, tapered pods point to the sky on plants that grow up to 6 feet tall. While most of the narrowly conical pods ripen to red, some are yellow, orange, or purple when mature. The nickname "bird's eye chili" refers to the preference birds have for this chile variety. Malaysians call the Thai chile pepper "chili padi" because it looks like the grains of the local rice.

The small pods have a pungent heat. The fruit has smooth, thin skin and weighs 2 to 3 grams each. The flowers are greenish or yellowish white. Thai chiles are widely hybridized and cultivated, resulting in many different types.

How to Serve or Use

Thai peppers have medicinal, culinary, and ornamental uses.

Thai chile is responsible for the fiery zing of much of Southeast Asian cuisine. Nearly all traditional Thai dishes used these chiles. Thai cooks use the larger dried whole chiles in curries. They soak the pods and remove the seeds before using to lessen the heat. Then they pound the seedless chiles with other spices to get the complex color and flavor of curry. The smaller chiles are not typically used in spice mixes.

Indians use Thai pepper in traditional dishes of the Kerala cuisine. It is the main ingredient in kochchi sambal, a Southeast Asian salad with fresh coconut ground with the chiles and seasoned with salt and lime juice. Thai chiles may also be pickled and served as a condiment. A popular sauce combines the chiles with garlic, vinegar, and salt. The Filipino dish called tinola uses the leaves.

Thai chiles have been used to ease arthritis and rheumatism. They may relieve flatulence, dyspepsia, and toothache. When mixed with water Thai chiles make a natural insect repellent and pesticide.

Plants cultivated for ornamental use feature a multitude of different colored pods at the same time. Ornamental peppers tend to be less pungent than varieties grown for eating, while some varieties have both ornamental and culinary uses.

Tien Tsin

Pronunciation: tin-tsin
Length: 1 - 2"
Width: ¼ - ½"
Scientific Name: Capsicum annuum
Other Names: tianjin pepper
Scoville Range: 50,000 - 75,000

Origin and History

The Tien Tsin chile derives its name from the Chinese province of the same name where the peppers were originally harvested. This pepper is now grown in many locations, including the United States. Once considered an exotic in the United States, it is increasingly available at Asian markets in this country.

Description

This very hot and shiny bright red chile has a slender shape like the cayenne pepper. The fruits, which mature from green to red, point upward on the bush. Sun dried pods are so light in weight, it takes dozens of pods to make one ounce. The plants produce relatively low yields.

The fruit has a pungent and musty flavor that imparts a spicy taste to food and is slightly reminiscent of Italian red pepper. The plentiful seeds are extremely hot and can overpower the flavor of the fruit; because of this some recipes recommend discarding the seeds.

How to Serve or Use

Tien Tsin chiles are very common in Asian cuisine. Among Chinese dishes it particularly lends itself to Hunan and Szechuan cooking styles. Dishes that use Tien Tsin peppers include, among many others, spicy Szechuan shrimp, curd rice (Asian Indian comfort food), lemon rice, and chicken curry in rice yogurt milk. Tien Tsin chile is an important ingredient in kung pao dishes, which combine chicken, seafood, or vegetables with peanuts in sesame sauce with hot chile paste and ginger.

Asian cooks sometimes add the whole pod to soups and stir-fry dishes and remove it before serving. Another way to use Tien Tsin chiles is to grind them into course flakes. Tien Tsin chiles also make a hot and toasty chile oil.

Contemporary Cajun and Creole cooking use Tien Tsin chiles to add heat to jambalaya, the traditional spicy meat, shellfish, and vegetable stew.

Tien Tsin is popular for making infused oil and the pepper's high staining capability results in a deep red colored oil.

YATSUFUSA

Pronunciation: yat-shu-FEW-sa
Length: 2 - 3"
Width: ¼ - 3/8"
Scientific Name: Capsicum annuum
Other Names: chilies japones
Scoville Range: 40,000 - 75,000

Origin and History

The hot specialty pepper yatsufusa originated in Japan. The name refers to a dwarf tree that does not grow into a larger one. Although Japan uses fewer chiles than other Asian countries, the yatsufusa pepper is a popular condiment in Japanese cuisine.

The peppers are planted in late spring and early summer and mature in 60 days. Yatsufusa peppers can be harvested before or after they are fully ripe. The young green peppers are picked directly from the branches. The mature peppers are left on their branches and the leaves are removed when harvested. The branches are hung until dry and then the peppers are removed.

Description

The yatsufusa grows from beautiful medium sized plants that have multiple branches and dark green foliage. The pepper grows out of the top of the plant in tight clusters along with yellow flowers. The peppers ripen from dark green to a deep red. The plant grows 18 to 24 inches tall.

Yatsufusa peppers are mild with a pleasant heat and a flavor like cayenne or Thai pepper. In Japanese cuisine they are considered as the flavor enhancement of a dish rather than additional heat.

How to Serve or Use

Yatsufusa peppers are used in Japanese dishes including stir fries, curries and soups. The young, green peppers are used when mild heat is needed for the dish. The mature peppers are hotter and typically used dried.

The peppers are used to make spicy hot sauces and rubs for smoked meat. Combining the ripe red peppers with the young green chiles brings out the best flavor.

SCOVILLE SCALE

Pepper	Scoville	Pepper	Scoville
Cherry	100 - 3,500	Aji	30,000+
Anaheim	500 - 2,500	Cayenne	30,000 - 50,000
Ancho	1,000 - 1,500	Tabasco	30,000 - 50,000
New Mexico	1,000 - 1,500	Guntur Sannam	35,000 - 40,000
Poblano	1,000 - 1,500	Santaka	40,000 - 50,000
Pasilla	1,000 - 2,000	Yatsufusa	40,000 - 75,000
Cascabel	1,000 - 5,000	Tien Tsin	50,000 - 75,000
Rocotillo	1,500 - 2,500	Korean	50,000 - 100,000
Chilaca	1,500 - 2,500	Thai	50,000 - 100,000
Guajillo	1,500 - 5,000	Bird's Eye	50,000 - 100,000
Mulato	2,500 - 3,000	Chiltepin	50,000 - 100,000
Mirasol	2,500 - 5,000	Dundicut	55,000 - 65,000
Kashmiri	2,500 - 5,000	Malagueta	60,000 - 100,000
Fresno	2,500 - 8,000	Habanero	100,000 - 350,000
Jalapeno	2,500 - 8,000	Scotch Bonnet	100,000 - 350,000
Chipotle	5,000 - 10,000	Pequin	100,000 - 400,000
Hungarian Yellow Wax	5,000 - 15,000	Fatalii	125,000 - 325,000
Serrano	10,000 - 25,000	Red Savina Habanero	350,000 - 580,000
Manzano	10,000 - 30,000	Naga Jolokia	850,000 - 1,000,000
Arbol (de Arbols)	15,000 - 60,000	Naga Viper	855,000 - 1,359,000

PHOTO CREDITS

Title Page and Introduction
www.flickr.com/photos/toofarnorth
www.flickr.com/photos/sfllaw

Aji
www.flickr.com/photos/pviojoenchile
www.flickr.com/photos/jkohen

Anaheim
www.flickr.com/photos/badcomputer
www.flickr.com/photos/niceness

Ancho
www.flickr.com/photos/50512402@N03

Arbol (de Arbols)
www.flickr.com/photos/notahipster
www.flickr.com/photos/puroticorico

Bird's Eye
www.flickr.com/photos/wwworks
www.flickr.com/photos/wwworks

Cascabel
commons.wikimedia.org/wiki

Cayenne
www.flickr.com/photos/nicmcphee

Cherry
www.flickr.com/photos/jronaldlee
www.flickr.com/photos/pzpz927

Chiltepin
www.flickr.com/photos/jcaldi

Chipotle
upload.wikimedia.org/wikipedia
www.flickr.com/photos/misbehave

Dundicut
en.wikipedia.org/wiki

Fatalii
commons.wikimedia.org/wiki

Habanero
www.flickr.com/photos/hoegsberg
www.flickr.com/photos/chokingsun

Hungarian Yellow Wax
http://www.flickr.com/photos/gregor_y

Jalapeno
www.flickr.com/photos/quazeck
www.flickr.com/photos/akeg

Korean
www.flickr.com/photos/naotakem/
www.flickr.com/photos/fotoecke

Malagueta
www.flickr.com/photos/tcelestino

Manzano
www.flickr.com/photos/lacatholique

Mirasol
www.flickr.com/photos/rob-sinclair

Mulato
commons.wikimedia.org/wiki

Naga Jolokia
www.flickr.com/photos/wstryder
www.flickr.com/photos/saucysalad

New Mexico
www.flickr.com/photos/nieve44
www.flickr.com/photos/puroticorico

Pasilla
www.flickr.com/photos/lacatholique

Pequin
www.flickr.com/photos/philip-ester
www.flickr.com/photos/potawie

Poblano
www.flickr.com/photos/dionhinchcliffe
www.flickr.com/photos/23126594@N00

Red Savina Habanero
www.flickr.com/photos/buggolo
www.flickr.com/photos/buggolo

Scotch Bonnet
www.flickr.com/photos/boinger
www.flickr.com/photos/beckayork

Serrano
www.flickr.com/photos/karinhodginjones
www.flickr.com/photos/ryustar

Tabasco
www.flickr.com/photos/davedehetre
upload.wikimedia.org/wikipedia

Thai
www.flickr.com/photos/azadam
www.flickr.com/photos/azadam

CPSIA information can be obtained
at www.ICGtesting.com
Printed in the USA
LVHW072139121020
668643LV00012B/1316